Dinosaur Detectives

Search for the Facts...

Tyrannosaurus and Other Cretaceous Dinosaurs

Tracey Kelly

BROWN BEAR BOOKS

Published by Brown Bear Books Ltd
4877 N. Circulo Bujia
Tucson, AZ 85718
USA

and

Leroy House
436 Essex Rd
London N1 3QP
UK

ISBN 978-1-78121-407-7

Library of Congress Cataloging-in-Publication Data available on request

Text: Tracey Kelly
Designer: John Woolford
Design Manager: Keith Davis
Editorial Director: Lindsey Lowe
Children's Publisher: Anne O'Daly
Picture Manager: Sophie Mortimer

Picture Credits
Public Domain: Connie Ma 4.

Brown Bear Books has made every attempt to contact the copyright holder.
If you have any information, please contact: licensing@brownbearbooks.co.uk

Manufactured in the United States of America
CPSIA compliance information: Batch#AG/5609

Websites
The website addresses in this book were valid at the time of going to press. However, it is possible that contents or addresses may change following publication of this book. No responsibility for any such changes can be accepted by the author or the publisher. Readers should be supervised when they access the Internet.

Contents

How Do We Know about Dinosaurs?

Scientists are like detectives.
They look at dinosaur fossils.
Fossils tell us where dinosaurs lived.
They tell us how big they were.

This *Tyrannosaurus* skeleton is named Sue. She is 67 million years old! Sue is the largest *Tyrannosaurus* ever found. She is 40 feet (12 meters) long.

How to Use This Book

This tells you what the animal ate.

Plant-eater

Meat-eater

These tell you when the animal lived.

This shows you how big the animal was.

A map shows you where the first fossils were found.

Read on to become a dinosaur detective!

What Was Earth Like?

Tyrannosaurus lived in the Cretaceous period. That was more than 65 million years ago. The land was dry. But rivers flowed through it. They were full of fish. Plants grew near the water.

Argentinosaurus

Say it! (AR-jen-TEEN-oh-SAW-rus)

Argentinosaurus was a giant plant-eater. It had a long neck! It ate tons of food every day. It plodded slowly on four huge legs.

MINI FACTS

Argentinosaurus lived in herds. The young were in the middle. That kept them safe.

FACT FILE

NAME: *Argentinosaurus* means "Argentine lizard"

WEIGHT: 55–100 tons (50–100 metric tons)

FOOD: plants and tree leaves

HABITAT: evergreen forests

First found in ...
Argentina, 1987

Baryonyx

Say it! (BAR-ee-ON-icks)

Baryonyx was a meat-eater. It ate fish, too! It caught them with its sharp claws.

MINI FACTS
Baryonyx's claws were 12 inches (35 cm) long!

FACT FILE

NAME: *Baryonyx* means "heavy claw"

WEIGHT: 1.5–2.2 tons (1.4–2.0 metric tons)

FOOD: fish and meat

HABITAT: forests and meadows around rivers, lakes, and swamps

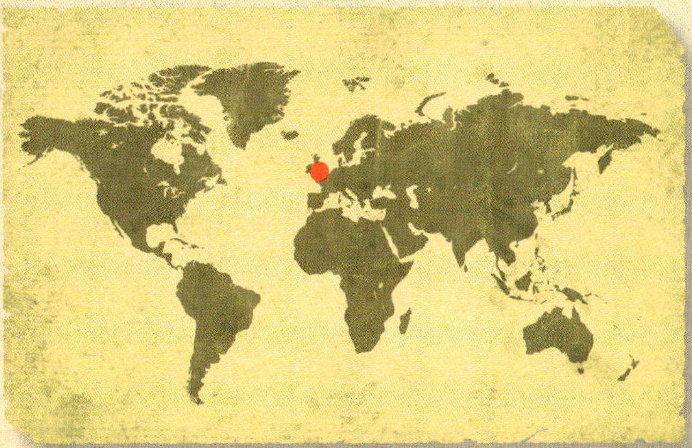

First found in ...
England, 1983

Gallimimus

Say it! **(GAL-ee-MEE-mus)**

Gallimimus looked like an ostrich.
But it had a tail! It lived in small herds.
It could see very well.

MINI FACTS

Galliminus **could run up to 43 miles (69 km) per hour. That's as fast as a car!**

FACT FILE

NAME: *Gallimimus* means "chicken mimic"

WEIGHT: 970 pounds (440 kg)

FOOD: small animals, insects, plants, eggs

HABITAT: near rivers, streams, and shallow lakes

First found in ...

Mongolia, 1963

Iguanodon

Say it! (ig-WAH-no-don)

Iguanodon was a plant-eater.
It grabbed plants with its beak.
Iguanodon had big thumb spikes.
It could stab other dinosaurs!

MINI FACTS

Iguanodon was the second dinosaur to be named.

FACT FILE

NAME: *Iguanodon* means "iguana tooth"

WEIGHT: about 3.4 tons (3.1 metric tons)

FOOD: plants

HABITAT: swampy places, plains, forests, mountains, deserts, and beaches

First found in ...
England, 1822

Oviraptor

Say it! (OH-vih-RAP-tor)

Oviraptor was as fast as an ostrich!
It had three fingers on each hand.
Oviraptor had a powerful beak.
It could crack open hard food.

MINI FACTS

Oviraptor laid eggs in a nest. It sat on its nest to guard the eggs.

FACT FILE

NAME: *Oviraptor* means "egg hunter"

WEIGHT: 77 pounds (35 kg)

FOOD: hard fruits, nuts, eggs, and possibly shellfish

HABITAT: deserts and dry areas

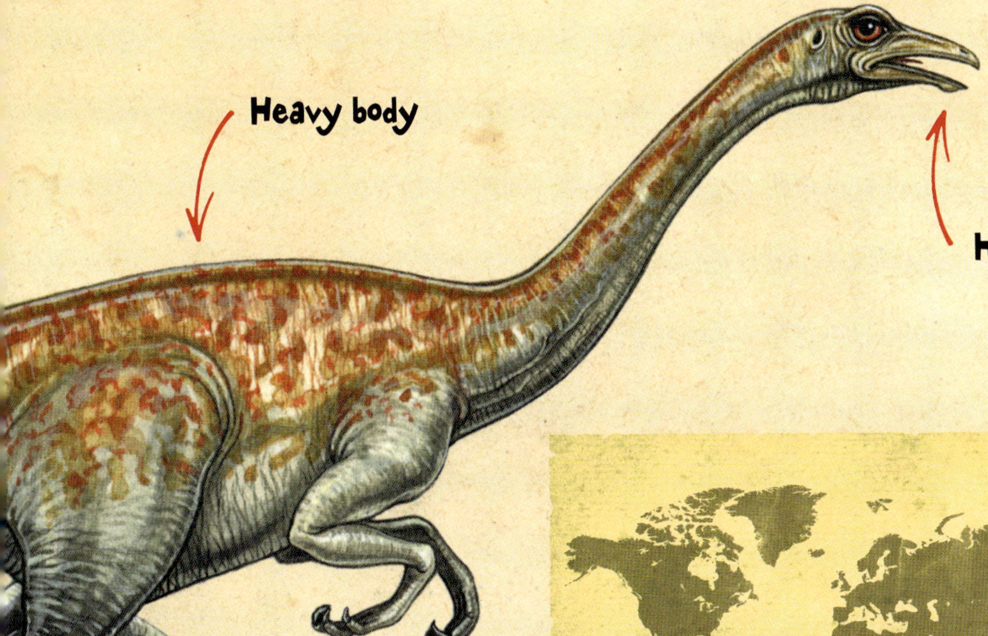

First found in ...

Mongolia, 1923

Triceratops

Say it! **(try-SER-ah-TOPS)**

Triceratops was a massive plant-eater. Its head had three horns. It had a bony neck frill. *Triceratops* lived in North America.

MINI FACTS

Triceratops had 400 to 800 teeth! It only used a few at a time.

FACT FILE

NAME: *Triceratops* means "three-horned face"

WEIGHT: 6 tons (5.4 metric tons)

FOOD: twigs and leaves

HABITAT: open woodlands

First found in ...

Denver, Colorado, 1887

Tyrannosaurus

Say it! (tie-RAN-oh-SAW-rus)

Tyrannosaurus was a fierce meat-eater. It had a bulky body. Its head was huge. But its arms were tiny.

MINI FACTS

Tyrannosaurus's teeth were the size of bananas!

FACT FILE

NAME: *Tyrannosaurus* means "tyrant lizard"

WEIGHT: 8 tons (7.3 metric tons)

FOOD: other dinosaurs

HABITAT: forests and land near rivers

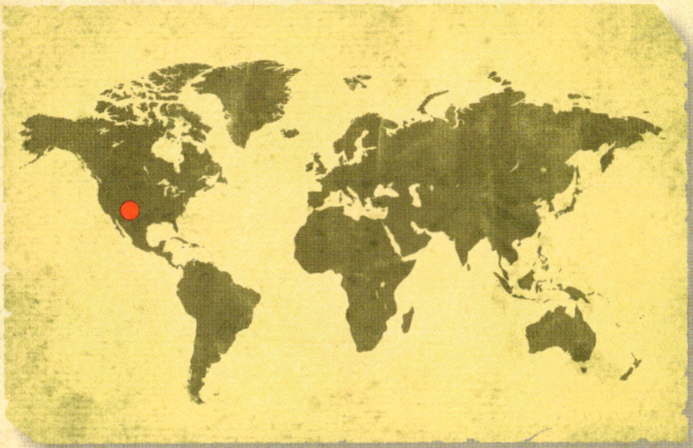

First found in ...

Colorado, 1874

Dinosaur Quiz

Test your dinosaur detective skills! Can you answer these questions? Look in the book for clues. The answers are on page 24.

2 Which dinosaur looked like an ostrich with a tail?

1 Which dinosaur caught fish?

3 Which dinosaur ate tons of food every day?

4 How did *Oviraptor* make its young?

Glossary

fossil

Part of an animal or plant in rock.
The animal or plant lived in ancient times.

habitat

The kind of place where an animal usually lives.

herd

A group of animals that lives together.

meat-eater

An animal that eats mostly meat.

plant-eater

An animal that eats only plants, not meat.

Find out More

Books

The Big Book of Dinosaurs, DK Editors (DK Children, 2015)

Everything Dinosaurs: Chomp on Tons of Earthshaking Facts and Fun (National Geographic Kids), Blake Hoena (National Geographic, 2014)

Websites

discoverykids.com/category/dinosaurs/

www.kids-dinosaurs.com/cretaceous-dinosaurs.html

naturalhistory.si.edu/exhibits/backyard-dinosaurs/

Index

Quiz Answers: 1. *Baryonyx* caught fish with its sharp claws. **2.** *Gallimimus* looked like an ostrich. **3.** *Argentinosaurus* ate tons of food every day. **4.** *Oviraptor* laid eggs in a nest and sat on them.